HUMBERSTONE

as I remember it

Edited by Kevin Turner

Thatched Cottage. Early 1920's

Published 1991. Leicestershire Libraries and Information Service,
99 Burleys Way, Leicester LE1 3TZ

Printed by Echo Press, Loughborough.

ISBN 085 022 306 7

Introduction

"Humberstone As I Remember it" is the eighth title in the ever popular series published by Leicestershire Libraries and Information Service. It is based on the entries received in the "Humberstone as I remember it" competition run during the summer of 1991. The competition asked for memories of Humberstone before 1950.

Of the 46 entries received, 40 were written and six were taped. The job of the judges was made enjoyable, if difficult, by the overall quality of the entries which was very high, and although a clear winner and four runners up did emerge the marking was close. The competition asked for personal memories of the area and did not insist on historical accuracy. The booklet is the same, and although the spelling of names and places has occasionally been corrected, the "facts" have not. Some of the reminiscences are from after 1950, but I have left them in if they bring the story up to date. What we were trying to obtain was a picture of life in a village on the borders of Leicester up to the 1950's and the changes that were apparent even then.

One question thrown up by the competition was where does Humberstone begin and end? Our first thoughts were that it covered old Humberstone Village and the Garden City, but quite a few entrants wrote about West Humberstone, "New" Humberstone or the Uppingham Road area. The majority of the entries and most of the booklet conform to our original boundaries, but the best entries relating to "New" Humberstone and the Uppingham Road have also been included.

The first part of the book is made up of the winning entries, which are published in their entirety. Other complete entries have been included where they say something original or illustrate a particular aspect of life that has since disappeared. This is followed by extracts from most of the remaining entries grouped together by subject. The last section covers New Humberstone and Uppingham Road.

Old Humberstone, late 1920's

Acknowledgements.
The people who entered the competition for providing such an interesting collection of reminiscences.

Paul Leivers, Area Librarian, St Barnabas Area, and all the staff especially at St. Barnabas and Humberstone Libraries for their help, interest and encouragement.

Radio Leicester and the local papers; Leicester Mercury, Humberstone Mail and Leicester Mail for their help publicising the competition.

My fellow judges Miss Stead and Mr Cooper. Without their knowledge of Humberstone the judging would have been much more difficult. They both lead busy lives and have other demands on their valuable time, which makes me all the more grateful for their help.

Everyone who submitted photographs for the booklet or gave permission for the use of photographs.

Kim for her patience and help.

Last, but not least Hannah.

Aerial photograph of Humberstone . 1930's (Kindly loaned by Miss M Hunt)

The winning entry was submitted by Mrs Margery Harrold, who was born in Stanley Drive in 1928. She was married at St. Mary's Church in 1951. She has worked as a secretary and shorthand typist and was a clerical assistant at a childrens home for mentally handicapped children before retiring. Her interests include watercolour painting, gardening and playing the organ. She gives us an affectionate picture of childhood in the village of Humberstone through the 1930's.

"I remember the Humberstone of my childhood as a village in the true sense of the word. I was born a twin in Stanley Drive in a house built on land which once belonged to Humberstone Hall. Incidentally Pine Tree Avenue was the original drive to the hall. By the time my grandparents bought the land the hall was no longer in existence. Before the house was built my grandparents, who were business people, had erected a wooden bungalow as a weekend retreat. Other houses were soon to follow and gradually Stanley Drive was more or less as it is today.

I remember my childhood days as a very happy time. I was born in 1928 and the second world war was eleven years away. As children we were never at a loss for things to do. The fields were only just over a stile behind the church. The Lido swimming pool at 6d a time was at the bottom of the road. Fourpennyworth at the Trocadero Cinema was always a treat on a Friday night. The seasons brought different games throughout the year - whip and top, marbles, skipping, snobs, hoops, and card throwing etc. Then after dark there was always "lurky" with the telegraph pole as the "home" post. We also had a large long garden, where at the first sign of sun out came the kitchen table and meals were "al fresco" in the garden. Our house was always open house for the hordes of relatives who used to devour my mother's wonderful cooking whenever the "City" played their team.

Now to the "village". The large house on the corner of Main Street which now houses the British Legion, was owned by a Mr Lewin who had a daughter with Downs Syndrome who could often be seen sitting on a swing in the garden, who, to my shame we nicknamed hou-hou.

Further along Main Street was a shop called Underwoods. This was a general store selling groceries and almost everything else. There was also Mr Pick the cobbler on this side of the street. Next came some cottages where Mr Cross lived who ran the local garage over the road, where we were sent with 6d and the accumulator to be charged for Dad's cat's whisker radio. Also in these cottages lived the great (in all senses of the word) Mrs Smith whose ample proportions were always hidden

Main Street. 1920's

by a large print overall. She was a real character and would always be seen having a chat with someone or other. Then came the Windmill pub and the old Church Hall.

On the other side of Main Street was the old Plough Inn, the blacksmith's shop and a house where Mr Hurd the caretaker/verger of St. Mary's Church lived. I believe somewhere along this side was a fish shop and then there was a haberdashery and knitting wool shop first owned by Glad Wren and in later years by Mrs Rose Vyse.

Then came Bartram's the butchers and then a rough road led down to Cross's garage and the Liberal Hall where my parents spent many happy hours at whist drives and dances, and as we grew older we were allowed to go too. My mother once won a cut glass and silver cruet set which was presented to her by Elsie and Doris Waters, who I presume must have been appearing at the Leicester Palace.

At the corner of Main Street and Vicarage Lane was the post office and general grocer's latterly owned by the Allison Family. There was also Mr Hall's sweet shop.

We were Methodists but as young children we always attended Good Friday services at St Mary's as hot cross buns were handed out! We attended Humberstone School and many is the time we only just arrived for the bell as the recreation ground was built at the back of the school and we made a detour through the "recky".

We were usually given a halfpenny to spend at Mr Hall's sweet shop on the way back to school after lunch or sometimes half an orange. My first teacher was Miss Attenborough and we learnt to write on slates and no computers or calculators in those days, we learnt to count with small round shells. Some of the other teachers who come to mind were Dicky Palmer, Miss Wilmhurst, Edwin Smith, Miss Reesby, and a lovely lady called Miss Draycott, who when my twin won a certificate and I didn't, bought me a little sewing set in a pretty chintz box. Mr Nobby Clarke was headmaster and Mr Duffin the hard working caretaker. In our class there were four sets of twins and my sister and I were never parted in all the years we were at Humberstone School.

Money was always in short supply but there was often a penny for the "stop me and buy one" ice cream man on his three wheel bicycle. We also always had our "Saturday Penny" to spend in the village and would often meet up with a group of patients from the Towers also spending their pocket money.

I will always have happy memories of Sunday evening walks around Humberstone and also the claypits on Thurmaston Lane and of looking for the Humber Stone. I only hope it retains some of the village atmosphere for future generations."

The first runner-up was Mr G P Hall. Mr Hall moved to Humberstone with his parents when he was 3 years old. He attended Humberstone School before going on to the City Boys School at Humberstone Gate. He married his wife, Jayne, in 1961. After 31 years working in various capacities for George Durston & Son, he retired and now lives in Hythe on the edge of the New Forest, overlooking the Solent. It is purely by chance that he was in Leicester on the day of the Radio Leicester broadcast.

"One of my earliest recollections as a small child is watching an engine shunting wagons into the sidings by the coal wharf at the back of the houses on Kitchener Road. The station master's house was at the bottom of Kitchener Road with the entrance to the coal wharf just behind it (where the health centre now stands) and a bridge carried the railway over Uppingham Road. Humberstone station was on the opposite side of Uppingham Road and, although about a mile from old Humberstone village, it was near what was until the 1920's the end of the built up area. The old tram lines had a link near Duxbury Road and this was the remains of the original tram terminus. Incidentally the correct name of St. Barnabas Church is St. Barnabas, New Humberstone.

The railway from Belgrave Road station carried a regular train service to Humberstone and on to Thurnby and Scraptoft, Ingarsby, Lowersby, and John O'Gaunt. It crossed Coleman Road bridge and passed behind the houses in Saltersford Road, then between Humberstone Park and Wicklow Drive, crossing under Uppingham Road diagonally at the Goodwood Road-Colchester Road crossroads. The train service was gradually reduced and the "Thurnby Flier" as it was often called, ended in 1957, but the popular Skegness excursions continued until September 1962. The line closed to goods traffic in 1964, and the bridge was removed and station demolished in 1968.

Another childhood memory of mine was of watching for the lamplighter on his walk down Humberstone Drive at dusk. I used to see him from home on Tennis Court Drive while looking across the small spinney at the back which belonged to Mr Fred Wale. The spinney and old cottage were cleared in 1957 to make way for the Hayling Crescent development in 1962. While the newer roads were lit by electricity, Humberstone Drive was still lit by gas lamps. It was formerly the main road to the village in the days of Humberstone Hall. Tennis Court Drive was obviously the site of the tennis courts and Pine Tree Avenue at its lower end was the main entrance to the hall. The trees however are not pine trees but California Redwoods. I do not remember the hall but the stables and the outbuildings became the cottages at the end of Pine Tree Walk.

I attended Humberstone School from 1938 to 1944 and began in the wooden classroom of the Infant School, my first teacher being Miss Attenborough. I remember too from my early years at school the band sessions when we all had triangles and tamborines, presided over by Miss Stead. Miss Bennison was the head of the Infant School while the Junior Headmistress was Miss A A Quiney. Perhaps the best remembered teacher was the deputy head Mr D V "Pop" Crawley, but I still recall one of the characters of bygone Humberstone who taught at the school for many years, Miss Alice Draycott. Whenever I hear hymns being sung I still remember where I learnt many of them and picture the classroom at Humberstone School with Miss Draycott. Apart from the teachers at Humberstone I remember the popular caretaker, Mr Duffin, humping crates of milk bottles in each day and stoking up to keep the school warm.

Humberstone Park was always a great attraction, especially during the war years when I was young. I particularly liked the boats on the Thurnby Brook which passes through the park and we had the choice between

Humberstone Park. 1930's

canoes and small paddle boats. They were overseen by one man on the landing stage directly in front of the bowling green and there was good fun to be had in negotiating the s-bends and bridges. Apart from the boats there was often a band playing in the park and sometimes a concert party. The bowling green and tennis courts were in full use with plenty of spectators sitting around watching and more often than not a cricket match was taking place just beyond the brook. In spite of the war the park was always kept clean and tidy and was well used. Just across the road from the park stood the Trocadero Cinema which was another major attraction in the area. Not only was it the largest cinema in Leicester but it was also an ABC cinema showing the latest films exactly the same as the Savoy in Leicester. The Trocadero was built in the early 1930's by Bert Coles of Thurnby. It became a bingo hall in 1963 and sadly was destroyed by fire on September 8th 1967. The L-shaped ballroom in the dome at the front escaped the fire but the whole site was cleared to make way for flats and a petrol station as it is today.

Both Humberstone Park and the Trocadero were served by trams from Leicester, the tram terminus being near the bottom of Humberstone Drive. The trams were regular, frequent and reliable but slow and uncomfortable and I much preferred the buses which ran through Humberstone Village to the Garden City. Prior to 1938 a service was operated by the blue coaches of Harry Cleaver and Son of Green Lane Road before Leicester City Transport bought the route. On March 7th 1938 two services started. Route 37 from Leicester ran up Overton Road, which was a straight road through what has been renamed

Wycombe Road, to Humberstone Drive and Thurmaston Lane to a terminus a few yards short of Gipsy Lane, then round the triangle and back the same way. This service was discontinued when war broke out but route 36 which started on the same day continued throughout the war and beyond and was renumbered 37 in 1949, having been linked with the New Parks Estate service on 19th May 1947. I was fascinated by the buses which ran to the Garden City although through the war years the service was operated by one bus every forty minutes. The vehicles were brand new in 1939, very large 64 seater, six wheeled buses known to the crews as Queen Marys, and as far as I know they were the only ones of their type. I loved them and liked nothing better than to walk to the Garden City in order to enjoy the 1/2d ride back. In those days it was possible to walk up the very narrow Steins Lane and having passed the new Hungarton Boulevard, there was a footpath which led to the bottom of Lilac Avenue. The Garden City belonged to the Anchor Tenants Association and was a small community with a Co-op store in the centre and Laburnham Hall opposite for dances and meetings. The bus travelled along the full length of Keyham Lane and down Chestnut Avenue, which was the end of the built up area. It was pleasant to look across the fields towards Scraptoft Church in the distance, sometimes watching, according to season, the ploughing or the harvesting of ripened corn. The bus terminus was along Laburnham Road and the bus then returned to Keyham Lane via Fern Rise, which in those days was an unadopted road and resulted in a very bumpy ride. So in 1944 a concrete square was added to Laburnham Road at the bottom of Chestnut Avenue to enable the buses to return the way they came. Unfortunately the square was only just big enough for its purpose and there was nothing to prevent the bus from reversing over the edge. People waiting along the route were used to seeing the bus pass by full but it was most disconcerting to be told that there would be no bus because it had fallen down a hole!

Humberstone in the 1940's was remarkably quiet. Standing by the gate at home on Tennis Court Drive I often watched the bus go by and then followed it's progress by hearing it starting from the bus stops through the village all the way down Keyham Lane. There were very few cars owing to petrol rationing, yet I remember Mr Allison, the village post master, used to come out to direct the traffic at the top of Vicarage Lane when the school buses were due to come up from Goodwood Road. Main Street was very narrow then and I wonder how many people remember the stone fox on the wall of the Warren. Just beyond the Warren were the small shops of Mr Pick the shoe repairer, Underwood's the grocers and confectioners and next to that a hairdresser. Opposite the Warren was a long building used as a workshop, the Plough Inn, then Paddocks Yard with its row of thatched cottages. All of these made way for the Humberstone Pub in 1964. I remember the village blacksmith and more than once I watched him shoe a horse. The smithy was replaced by W S Earp cycle shop but the next row of shops are still there. No.21 was originally a fishmonger's but was later used by hairdresser Maurice Bottom, perhaps better known for the rescue and care of animals and birds. No.23 was draper Rose Vyse and in those days the shopkeeper was Mrs Vyse herself. Next came Mr Hall the greengrocer (no relation) and Bartram's the butchers, behind which was a garage. A row of terraced houses stood facing St. Mary's Church and fronting the very narrow road, Allison's the grocer's and the post office which was on the corner of Vicarage Lane. The houses were demolished at the end of the severe winter of 1963 to make way for shops.

The corner of Humberstone Drive and Main Street. Date unknown. The library is the second building up on Main Street. (Kindly loaned by Mr A T Stevens)

At the bottom of the Main Street hill next to the Conservative Club was Humberstone Library in an old building which began its days as a congregational chapel. The librarian was Mr Percy Smith and for two years from 1949 to 1951 I was his assistant, the opening hours being 6.30 to 8.00 pm on Monday, Wednesday and Friday only. This small building was heated by a stove in which a fire had been lit earlier by the cleaner with a firelighter and coal. When we arrived in the evening it usually needed to be filled up with coke and so long as it was burning well we were all warm. However there were many evenings when the chimney had become blocked and we had to carry on serving the customers amid so much smoke that we could hardly see the books on the opposite shelf. Most people saw the funny side of this and the library was well used in those pre-television days. They came not only to exchange books but also for a chat with those they may not see otherwise. Children played and made noise, dogs barked and no-one minded, especially when the vicar, the Reverend Percy Lidster came in and asked "Have you heard the latest yarn?" He was extremely well liked and was seldom without an audience for the stories he used to tell. The library was a great meeting place but the building has now been put to other use since the library was closed on March 10th 1984 and eventually moved elsewhere.

ST. MARY'S
HUMBERSTONE

* * *

Unveiling & Dedication

OF

WAR MEMORIAL
WINDOW AND
BRONZE TABLET

* * *

Sunday, November 7th, 1920

S. H. Jesson, Printer, Leicester.

Programme for Dedication Service at St.Mary's Church. (Kindly loaned by Mr A T Stevens)

From 1920 the vicar of Humberstone was the Reverend John Tarleton Hodgson. He had enjoyed a long incumbency, having succeeded the Reverend Eric Farrar, subject of Dean Farrar's famous book "Eric, or Little by Little". However by the time war broke out he was a very elderly gentleman and I remember he sometimes visited Humberstone School and looked in on the classes when I was there. He remained vicar until after the war ended, owing to the manpower shortage, and then retired to live in Stanley Drive. In 1946 the new vicar was the Reverend Percy Lidster, previously rector of St Andrews, Aylestone. He attracted large congregations during his time at St. Mary's, especially for evensong. He reasoned that if you give them a good sermon and a good sing they'll come, and so they did. Canon Lidster, as he became in 1954, was also an astute businessman and the parish still benefits from the building work for which he provided the necessary motivation more than forty years ago. The first need was to replace the uneconomic Monks Rest vicarage which was in need of repair and was far too large with many rooms that were never used. I remember hearing him speak of a cell where centuries earlier the monks had been able to spend the night as they journeyed across the great forests of Needwood and Charnwood on their way to Laundes Abbey, hence the name Monks Rest.

The vicar and two long serving church wardens Bill Rowell and George Farrands prompted the sale of the Monks Rest and all its land to

St. Mary's Church. 1948

Leicester City Council, the proceeds from which were sufficient to fund the purchase of a site on the opposite side of Vicarage Lane and the construction of a modern vicarage. It was 1957 when the new vicarage became available for occupation but while this project was in its early stages there arose an even greater need in the parish. The old church school (as it was before the council school was built) was the centre for church activities but it was a tremendous blow when this was discovered to be unsafe. It was all demolished except for one small room fronting Main Street, severely curtailing church activities. There was now an urgent need for a new church hall but little scope for holding fund raising events to pay for it even though the Warren was a popular venue for garden fetes in those early years. However it was largely due to the vicar's ingenuity that a long term loan and exchange of land was arranged with Ansells Brewery, owners of the Windmill Inn, which meant that the new hall could be built behind the Windmill Inn at the side of the church and when completed, the old school site became the Windmill's car park.

The official opening of the church hall took place on Saturday November 22nd 1958 by Mr E Foster of Ansells and the then Bishop of Leicester, the Right Reverend R R Williams. Long before this event took place, the parish was involved in yet more building work. In 1954 the Netherhall Estate began to grow, covering the land where, as a boy, I had seen the farmer at work and soon there was a need for a new church. It was dedicated to St. Elizabeth on 30th October 1959, with Canon Lidster as vicar and the Reverend P J Lafford the curate in charge. Canon Percy Lidster retired on October 1st 1962 and lived at Rothley until his death in 1980 at the age of 87, but it must surely be a measure of his popularity that he became one of the few people to have a road - Lidster Close - named after him during his lifetime. Now living far away from my native Humberstone I still recall the scene as it used to be. I know many changes have taken place. Things do change. They always will, but for me Humberstone Park and its paddle boats, the quiet village and garden city with its bus service, Humberstone School, the old library and St Mary's Church, these things will always be the essential ingredients of "my" Humberstone.

Mr E W Freeman, who will be 80 next year, retired 19 years ago at the age of 60. He spent many years working as an electrical engineer for the Corah Group and is still a Fellow of the I.E.E.I.E. He currently does voluntary work at the hospital, driving patients for operations etc. His entry covering the early history of the Garden City was the second runner-up.

"I, Ernest Freeman was born before the first world war at No.77 Keyham Lane, Garden City, Leicester.

Our house was part of the Anchor Tenants Association. The Anchor Tenants being a group of workers employed at the Anchor Co-op Boot and Shoe works in Asfordby Street, Leicester.

These employees contributed a percentage of their wages to form a building fund and eventually used it to finance and purchase a block of land about half a mile east of Humberstone village.

The society then built ninety nine houses which were let at a nominal rent to the Anchor employees, my dad being a founder member. It was a self contained community having all the sports facilities: bowling green, tennis courts, long alley skittles, cricket pitch and complete children's play area with swings and see-saws etc. There was a church and a shop, above which was a hall for concerts, dancing and other functions. There were various tradesmen who were also Anchor employees. Mr Law was the handyman. Having no central heating in those days coal fires were the norm, and my dad in his spare time was the chimney sweep, while Bill Duffin delivered the coal.

I remember Tom Bowerman had a Model T Ford lorry, which every

Main Street. 1920's

morning and evening doubled as the local bus service. This was arrived at by Tom Bowerman having a garage at the bottom of Fern Rise in which was located a block and tackle for lifting a fourteen seater bus body with seven seats a side and as many standing as could scramble on. The illumination for the bus was one flash light bulb. The procedure was that each afternoon around 4.30 the bus body was lowered on to the lorry and remained there overnight, ready to take passengers to Humberstone tram terminus with as many journeys as possible from 7am to 9am. The bus body was then removed from the lorry and Tom returned to his job as general carrier, until 4.30 in the afternoon.

I can remember as a lad going to the little church school in Main Street Humberstone. Mr Clarke was headmaster, and Mrs Roberts taught the infants. The school heating was a primitive coke stove, the teacher having to leave the lessons to make up the fire. I remember walking to school in all weather from Garden City, as it was known, four times a day.

Living at the corner of Lilac Avenue we had a row of apple trees all the way down the Avenue, so we always had plenty of apples, but it never stopped me scrumping with the other kids. I suppose everybody's apples tasted better than our own. However if we were caught the village bobby PC Swinfield, would scuff us around the ears with his gloves, which never did us any harm. The old village shops were the general store run by Mrs Underwood which always smelled of fire lighters and paraffin. Next door was the village shoe repairers owned by Mr Pick. Opposite the village street was the blacksmiths yard run by Mr Mason.

What few gas lamps there were, were lit and extinguished by Mr Payne with his lamplighter pole.

The vicar in those days was the Reverend Tarleton Hodgson and I remember as an infant we were marched hand in hand, little boys and girls to all the religious festivals.

The two local characters in the village that come to my mind were "Loz" Arnold and Billy Wood, who's father owned the local milk round. One of his milk maids was Flo Kinton with her milk bucket and gill measure. The milk churn was carried on the horse drawn cart (no bottles in those days). As kids we had to make our own pleasure, but those bygone days were happy."

Mr Tom Downs came to Leicester from Scotland in 1935 when he was 19 years old. He married his wife, Ivy, in 1938. He worked as an engineer with F. Pollard & Co., for 46 years, retiring in 1980. Now 76, his main interest is gardening. His entry was one of the few to discuss the war years in Humberstone. He was our third runner-up.

"Our young family moved to Wansbeck Gardens just after the war started in 1939. The houses had just been built. Some of us had back gates into the field at the side of Abbots Road now Hungarton Boulevard. Then it finished at Steins Lane. In the field was part of an old farm way. It was about 50 yards long with high hedges each side about 20 feet apart. At the top and on the east side of this field was a high bank. The south side had a tree leaning over the bank which made a good swing for the youngsters. The archaeologists uncovered the foundations of an old house and the banks were the remains of the moat. Still there I believe under the car park. The youngsters had a lot of fun helping on the dig.

We all had our A.R.P. duties and took turns to keep watch when the sirens went. Sometimes all night and then off to work in the morning. We could see across the town and often stood watching the flames from Coventry. I remember one night we had just put our baby to bed upstairs when the sirens went off. I raced upstairs as I could hear the planes and hear the bombs coming down. By the time I picked him up they had all exploded. They sounded as if they were in the street but they landed in the fields at Scraptoft. I believe there were some incendiaries in the fields at the back of the school. The land mines that blew up Victoria Park pavilion and Steel and Burks factory in St Saviours Road also blew the windows out of Lloyds Bank at Humberstone Park.

Rationing was always a problem. We started the Monks Rest Allotments. Some of us also kept a few hens and rabbits. One garden in the Garden City had a couple of pigs. One day I heard a great deal of shouting and swearing coming from the direction of Steins Lane. Looking up the old way in the field there was a large greyhound racing down. I hid in the hedge and jumped out as it came level. He dropped a lovely plump hen at my feet and ran off.

Blackout was always a problem. Our rear windows looked right up Abbots Road. We were often in trouble with our local warden for chinks of light showing.

An old story about Humberstone Village, my mother in law was brought up in Overton Road, her own name was Edith Harris. She died in 1970 at Keyham Lane aged 85. When she was ten or eleven she had to take her dad's dinner to him. He was a blacksmith in the village. She told us she hated going as all the local lads would sit on the wall round the duck pond. She had red hair and they called the usual names after her. Where was the duck pond?

One of my neighbours lived when young, in Pine Tree Avenue somewhere round about 1920-30. It was a muddy track then. When they were going anywhere special they would walk down in wellies or old shoes, and put their good ones on and hide the others in the hedge.

During the war we had the Yanks in camp at Scraptoft. Before they left for the front they had a practice drop. There were parachutes coming down everywhere. Next night they were in the Windmill and the Plough telling the tale - some with slings and some limping. They were a lively lot and a credit to their country. Come to think of it so were most of us.

After the Yanks left we had prisoners of war. They used to march them along Scraptoft Lane to the camp in Hamilton Lane. Towards the end of the war you could see the soldiers getting younger. By the end most were young boys or old men.

I was in the Home Guard, Sunday morning you were on parade for drilling or arms training. During the week you were on a rota for guard duty during the night, usually outside the works. Sometimes you would find yourself under the wings of a large Lancaster bomber. It was a long night. Another night it was at Leicester Magazine. We had a trench at the General Hospital with one Lewis Gun. I never found it anything like the TV programme."

Our final runner-up was Miss Margaret Hunt, who started work two days before the outbreak of World War Two. She has worked as a nurse at a number of residential schools away from Leicester, returning to Leicester in 1960. She retired in 1983. She had been preparing her family tree until she became fully occupied caring for her elderly mother, who died recently aged 93. Miss Hunt brought the aerial photograph of Humberstone to our attention.

"I was born in 1923. When six years old, my family moved from 15 Freeman Road North to 82 Tennis Court Drive, Humberstone. My father had the 4 bedroom house built by a local builder, Mr Carrall of Stanley Drive, for approximately £1,500! I attended the newly built Humberstone Council School until passing the scholarship examination for Alderman Newton Girls School. Mr Clark, the headmaster was a great disciplinarian. I can remember receiving a good whack of the cane for fighting the boys! Two teachers were Mr Smith and Miss Bracken, who gave us an excellent, if strict, education.

There was a small sand quarry opposite the school where we delighted to slide down at our peril, and a spinney behind the school where we enjoyed climbing trees. At the bend approaching the school was waste land and the boys would lie in wait to slash our legs with stinging nettles. We weren't always angels even then.

The Warren Lodge. 1925

Humberstone was indeed a village then and still a fairly close community which, alas, disappeared when the Netherhall Estate was built. The remains of Humberstone Hall, home of the Pagets, were at the top of Pine Tree Avenue. We used to play amongst the large stones and rubble. The houses opposite us were built a little later. At the bottom of our garden was a paddock and the old coachman's cottage, which was still there when I left Humberstone in 1968 and had access to Humberstone Drive.

On turning right into the village at the top of Tennis Court Drive, on the left was the "Warren", a big house with a stone animal over the gateway. I remember attending a fete in the grounds. Bungalows were built in the grounds in the 1960's. Beyond this the pavement was built of "petrified kidneys", stones laid edge on. There was a dim cobbler's shop with an old latched door and Underwoods, a general grocery store, where excellent "mystery bags", price 1/2d, and "dab and suckers" could be purchased. Outside was a mounting block and a ring to tether a horse. The Windmill and its yard stood behind. Across the access to fields was the Church Hall and St. Mary's Church, the vicar being the Reverend Tarleton Hodgson, a gentleman of the old school. Being non-conformists we were not of his flock.

At the right-hand corner of Tennis Court drive and the Main Street was a large house belonging to the Lewin family. The British legion are now housed there. Further along was the old Plough Inn sited closer to the road than the present Humberstone Inn. Next was a court with old cottages, then the blacksmith's forge and yard. We were fascinated watching the blacksmith, a Mr Mason I believe, and his son shoeing horses. Later they turned to wrought iron work and it eventually became a bicycle shop. There was then a row of shops. I remember fish and chips, a dress and haberdashery shop called "Rose Vyse" and my favourite sweet shop Hall's. Mr Hall waited patiently whilst I spent most of my pocket money, 3d a week. Jelly babies, aniseed balls, liquorice sticks and gobstoppers were my favourites. There was also a butcher's shop called Bartram's. A road ran up the side of Bartram's leading to a very basic garage and petrol pumps. Before the post office at the corner of Vicarage Lane, where reigned a Mr. Simpkin, a rather unapproachable man, was a row of cottages. Around the corner from the church was the Manor where dwelt Dr. Ingram. Turning left from Tennis Court Drive down Main Street hill and past the thatched cottage on the corner there was Browning's builder's yard, the library and Conservative Club. Thurmaston Lane was not built until the early 30's and the only way to Thurmaston was via Gipsy Lane, where I didn't encounter any gypsies but plenty of harmless old tramps.

During the day we saw mostly tradesmen. These included Mr Heggs, the kind milkman wearing breeches and gaiters with his horse and trap carrying a huge churn and measure. A large white and blue jug was always ready to take the frothy, creamy milk (none of your semi-skimmed) which was placed on the cold thrall in the larder with a muslin cover complete with beads. No fridges in those days. Mr Pitcher was the baker with his big wooden tray of bread and sticky cakes (we were allowed bought cakes on Saturdays only), then Mr Boat, the greengrocer, with his pony and small dray, the coalman with his shire horse, always decorated on May day with brasses and ribbons. Hill's the grocers and the Corona man who was the last to be motorised. Plenty of manure for the enthusiastic gardeners! Occasionally the rag and bone man came along with his cry of "rag/bone". He didn't do much business but seemed to survive. The butcher and paper boys always whistled when delivering on their special bicycles. The whistle seems to have gone out of people these days. Anything and everything seemed to have been delivered in those days, even the postman made a delivery on Christmas Day.

Abbots Road. Early 1920's

It is inconceivable that we played street games on a road that is so busy now ie skipping, whip and top, hot rice, statues, lurky etc. etc. Hop scotch and marbles were also favourites and sledging down Greenland Drive in the winter, conkers in the autumn. We were never bored in those days before television. Plenty to do indoors and out, mostly making our own amusement with our friends.

When I came to Humberstone, the only means to get into town by public transport was the tram car, which started outside Humberstone Park where incidentally, we spent many happy hours on the swings and in the paddle boats on the brook pretending to be deaf when the attendant called "come in number 5". The bigger boys had canoes. The tram car stop was called "The Terminus". I notice that Pallant's, the newsagents, are still flourishing there, the first shop I remember when I lived in Freeman Road North and from where I purchased my "Chicks Own" paper. The house my father purchased in Freeman Road North was new and I can remember the lamplighter still coming round to light the gas lamps. Maycrofts was a sweet shop next to the park and opposite Wand's, the chemist. Gradually more shops were built. I remember the Co-op with sawdust on the butcher's department floor. Payment was made by wooden overhead cash carriers on cables, which intrigued me. The Trocadero Cinema and the Lido were built by Bert Cole after we moved to Tennis Court Drive. I believe they had stage acts apart from films in the early days. The first films I saw there were entitled "Africa Speaks" and "A Yank at the court of King Arthur". At certain times they had the "twopenny rush" where children could get in cheaply but sat on the front rows. Alas a fire broke out many years later at the Troc. after it had become a bingo hall and now, nothing left but a petrol station.

A bus service, Cleavers, was started from Humberstone in the 1930's. The bus was driven by Harry Cleaver, who used to sound his horn and wait for the regulars if they didn't appear. I think that my fare was 1.1/2d into town. Now there is a citybus, probably more efficient but I think with nostalgia of the days when Cleavers' rather rickety light blue bus went bouncing down Tennis Court Drive.

Top end of Gipsy Lane, looking towards Main Street.

I left Humberstone in 1941 and didn't return until 1960 and finally left in 1968. Some of the magic seemed to have gone from the place, but I was probably looking through a child's rose-coloured spectacles at those happy days of the early 1930's. Britain was still a great power and the shadow of war had not yet cast it's gloom. My sister, brother and I came from a very caring household with good friends and neighbours and were probably more privileged than some children, which cushioned the fact that it was the time of recession. I am sure that there was poverty under the surface in Humberstone, but people were slow to acknowledge that they were poor. I remember that we collected at school for a food hamper at Christmas to send to a poor family in one of the cottages. The mother was a proud woman and the boys were always neatly dressed with shining boots.

It may be that the close community of the village started to disintegrate when the Hall was pulled down and we newcomers arrived. I haven't been back to Humberstone for some years but I hope that there is still a community spirit and Humberstone has not lost its individuality. Meanwhile I shall remember Humberstone as it was with my rose-coloured spectacles. I wonder whether the chestnut trees still overhang Main Street?

Humberstone Station - A Booking Clerk's Story

Mr Leonard Woolley submitted this entry, and although it was not one of the winners it was thought interesting enough to include it all. Humberstone station was on the edge of Humberstone and many people have fond memories of using it. Mr Woolley gives us the other side of the story.

"On April 5th 1939 I was appointed Booking Clerk at Humberstone Station, LNER. and apart from a break of three months in Head Office, was there until April 1941. At that time, the station came under the supervision of Mr Langford, the Station Master at Thurnby and Scraptoft, who came over once a day to see that everything was in order and then back to Thurnby by bus. Thus the station was effectively run by the porter-signalman, Bob Forsyth, two lad porters, Ken Stevenson and Billy Holland and myself, a happy team.

Humberstone Station. 1957. (By kind permission of Leicestershire Museums, Art Galleries and Records Service)

Humberstone station was built on an embankment, and although the office and waiting rooms etc. were of brick construction, the platforms were of timber. We had an unusual advantage at Humberstone Station over the trams (which of course were running at that time) as it was cheaper to go by train to Leicester, Belgrave Road than by tram. We had quite a number of regular passengers each morning who worked at the British United Shoe Machinery Co. on Belgrave Road, who caught the morning train to Leicester - price three half-pence - whereas the tram to the same point was 2.1/2d and it was quicker by rail! - and no changing at the Clock Tower.

The trains were handy when the Flower Show and other functions were being staged at Abbey Park. We also booked tickets for Leicester, for excursions to Skegness. Humberstone folk could buy a ticket from us for use from Leicester especially for Sunday five-shilling trips each Sunday to Skegness. I have booked up to 200 passengers at a time and the Humberstone people would join the train at Belgrave Road and no queueing!

During the summer we also had an occasional Sunday School special train. One I remember was St Barnabas Sunday School Outing. This was to a station along the line - I think it was Lowesby. Never before or since have I seen so many youngsters and the excitment was at fever-pitch. We had to hold them in a long queue down the ramp leading to the platform - we daren't let them run about on the platform itself before the train came in. However they all got in safely and our little station staff was there to welcome them on return. All the children had a good time and came back loaded with bags of fruit, sweets and a stick of rock. I am sure there must be people around today who will remember.

The main business at Humberstone Station was the coal traffic. There was very little central heating about in 1939 and I think practically every house in Humberstone was supplied with coal from the station. Two of the biggest coal merchants were John Glover and the Leicester Co-op Society. John Glover even had his own fleet of railway wagons!

Just before the war broke out in 1939 Ken Stevenson had joined the Territorials and with the outbreak of war was called up. He came home on leave and also survived Dunkirk, but was taken prisoner by the Japanese and was on the prison ship that was sunk by the allies. Billy Holland transferred to the Loco Department and eventually became an engine driver. Bob Forsyth stayed at Humberstone until he retired and I became a relief Station Master and eventually retired to Scotland.

The Station Master's house at Humberstone was occupied by Mr Sam Cooper who became a Lord Mayor of Leicester.

The following recollection was put on tape by Mrs E Blankley. It is one of the earliest recollections that we received. It tells us something about the social life of the gentry and the domestic life of the staff of the old Hall.

Cottages nearest the estate. About 1920.

My father went to be groom for Sir Maurice Levy. There was a head groom, my father and two stable boys and we went to live in Steins Lane just outside the village, in a little thatched cottage with four rooms, two up and two down. It was in a cobble-stone yard and there was a pump in the middle of the yard where they all got water from and the toilets were at the top. There were two toilets, one for children and one for grown-ups and they were pans, there were no flush toilets. There was no gas laid on, we had to have paraffin lamps and candles for light. At the top of the lane it was all farm land and fields There was a brook in one field and a spring where watercress used to grow. I used to go to the village school, Sunday School and the church. I did win one or two prizes - they were books. Mr Paget presented us with them one year.

Keyham Lane. 1925.

We used to have a Sunday School treat and we used to walk to the fields at Barkby or Keyham. We used to have races and games and if we won a race, the girls would get a hair ribbon or a slide and the boys would get a handkerchief or a pencil. Then at about 3 o'clock a man with a float would come with a tea urn and homemade lemonade, and packets with tea in - there used to be a sticky bun and some biscuits with icing on and a jam sandwich - that was your tea. Every now and again the patients from Towers hospital, which we used to call the asylum, used to have a walk and they used to call into Mrs Towers shop, buy sweets and on their way back they would go past our cottages with the nurses. They used to go and sit in a ring in the field where the brook was. We children used to go and follow them. There used to be me, Laurie Glover and Jessie Laxton. One of the ladies called me over once, and I was a bit frightened but one of the nurses said you'll be alright and she gave me an aniseed ball. She asked me what my name was and what I did at school and I told her.

Leicester Mental Hospital, now the Towers Hospital. Early 1920's.

Once a year they had a charity ball at the asylum and all the gentry used to go and after the ball I used to go to the hall. The cook sent for me and the gardener's little girl and we would sit in the kitchen while she told us what the Levy girls had worn. They used to have long gloves which they had to button up and they had a little book with a pencil on their wrist and the gentlemen would put their names down at the side of the dances that they wished to have with the ladies. Lady Dorothy, well Miss Dorothy we always called her, her book was nearly always full, but the other daughter's wasn't and I suppose evidently Miss Dorothy was a bit more popular. The cook told us all this while we were having tea with the kitchen maid, the scullery maid used to come down to listen as well and it was really wonderful. If we had a bad cold or a cough we couldn't afford to pay for the doctor, his name was Dr Berridge, so we would take an empty bottle to the vicarage and they gave us some cough medicine - I think it was the five oils, it was a mauvey mixture and it was sweet.

Sir Maurice used to buy all our shoes. There were button up boots for the girls and lace ups for the boys, but they were so strong they used to make blisters on my heels. So my dad happened to mention this to Sir Maurice when he was talking to him and he made a special effort to get me some little shoes that were a bit softer - I wasn't very old, only about five or six."

Humberstone Hall

"I remember Humberstone around about mid 1935. As a small boy I used to visit my grandmother's house, who lived in a cottage next door to the Humberstone Constitutional Club, at the bottom of Main Street, Humberstone.

8 THE LEICESTER MERCURY, TUESDA

Lived 25 Years In Shilling A Year Cottage

HUMBERSTONE WOMAN'S DEATH

MRS. KATE TEMPLAR, of Old Humbersone, who has died at the age of 77, was the oldest woman Conservative in the village, and by an unusual gift she lived in a picturesque thatched cottage for 25 years for 1s. a year.

Her husband, Mr. George Templar, was head gardener to the Pagets at Humberstone Hall, and when Mr. Templar died they left Mrs. Templar the cottage during her life for a nominal rental as a token of their esteem for her husband's service.

Firmerly Village Nurse

Many years ago Mrs. Templar was the village nurse of Humberstone.

She had eight children. Two sons were killed on the same day in the Great War.

The shilling a year cottage

Cutting from the Leicester Mercury. 1938. (Supplied by Mr A T Stevens)

My grandfather, Mr George Templer, worked as head gardener for the Pagets of Humberstone Hall, and when he died in 1913 the cottage in which they lived was left to my grandmother for as long as she lived for 1 shilling a year by the Paget family.

The entrance to the Estate. Early 1900's.

The cottage in which she lived was actually two cottages side by side but with no connecting door, which seems remarkable in this day and age. There was a blue brick pathway between the two cottages in the back garden, where she would sort of pick her way at night in the pitch dark to her sleeping quarters in the little house as she called it, next door. The garden, as I remember it was filled with Victoria plums, Sweating apples, raspberries and an abundance of flowers and lilac trees, and in the summer evenings the sound of the church bells was a wonderfull sound and I can still remember it today."

"The Hall had a lovely old clock on it which used to chime every hour."

"The Hall Estate was the area bounded by Main Street, Vicarage Lane, Scraptoft Lane and Humberstone Drive. Humberstone Hall was in the centre, where Sir Maurice Levy lived, one of the partners of "Hart and Levy" clothing manufacturers whose factory was on Humberstone Road near Wimbledon Street. The Hall was situated at the top of what is now Pine Tree Avenue and I believe part of what was the laundry still remains.

Humberstone Drive, leading to the Estate. 1908. (Kindly loaned by Miss M Hunt)

The house called the Warren opposite Tennis Court Drive was lived in by Mr Myhill a hosiery manufacturer whose factory was at the corner of Nedham Street, his chauffeur lived in the thatched cottage opposite the Warren. A white five bar gate was across what is now Tennis Court Drive and "No Access" was allowed. Stanley Drive, Tennis Court Drive and Greenland Drive and Avenue did not exist."

"Humberstone Hall, at the back of my house was knocked down and large lumps of masonry lay amongst the shrubberies. My special cronies and I made pretend houses there and played hide and seek."

Contributors: Mr Stevens, Mrs JE Brewin, BM Purdy, Mrs L Wakelin.

The Manor House

"After the first world war when my dad came home, he married my mum who was from Melton Mowbray - she was in service in London Road, Leicester. My dad got a gardener's job at the "Manor House". Dr and Mrs Crosby lived there at the time. They had two sons, George and Vivian. Later George became a doctor and Honourable Physician to the Queen, and Vivian was a well known rugby player. The Manor house was a lovely house. I was three months old when I first went to stay there. The Crosby family used to take their holidays at their cottage in Norfolk, and we used to stay in the house while they were away.

There was a cellar in the house - the door leading down was at the end of the hall with stone steps down with a slight twist, then at the bottom was a wooden frame wide door, covered with wire mesh - this led to the church. When I got a bit older and a bit more daring, I opened the wire mesh door and stepped inside. I took a few steps, but it was dark, damp and had plenty of cobwebs, then I heard a voice shout "Kathleen!". My dad only called me Kathleen when I was in trouble. The tunnel from the manor to the church did exist. It was in Dr Darke's time it was blocked up.

The gardens to the Manor were lovely. Tennis court, croquet lawn, sunken garden with a sundial, kitchen garden, flowers and fruit trees. We used to put apples in a barrel, cover them with cork bits from grape boxes and send them to a children's home. Also in the gardens were peaches and grape vines, in a big glass house that used to be near the church mud wall. There was also a glass house for tomatoes and cucumbers.

Both these had coke fire heating and had to be kept burning during cold weather, day and night. I had to take my turn at stoking up,and I hated this job. I had to walk down from Scraptoft footpath, up the cobbled yard at the Manor, round by the potting shed, and walk close to a brick wall where frogs had made their home (when you hear hundreds of frogs croaking - you never forget it). On the other side of this wall was a field where at one time they kept highland cattle. There was a big black barn there which was destroyed by a German firebomb during the second world war.

Dr Crosby, Dr Garratt, Mr Myhill and my dad all used to go shooting and come back with braces of pheasants. These would be hung in the outside larder at the manor until they were "high" which means almost walking, it put me off pheasant for life.

After the death of Dr Crosby, Mrs Crosby and her sons left the village. Then came Dr Ingram with his wife and son and daughter, Nornie and Barbara. Barbara was about my age so we became good friends along with Fred Simkin, son of the village postmaster (Fred was killed on active service during the last war). Nornie Ingram became a doctor and later took a practice in the south of England. Barbara joined the ATS during the war. My dad had taught them both to drive, but not me, he wouldn't teach me. Barbara was awarded the BEM during the war.

Bonfire night was always a highlight at the manor. A big bonfire in the yard, with roast chestnuts, parkin, jacket potatoes and I was allowed to have a box of fireworks costing 2s 6d.

I remember one day, we kids, Nornie, Barbara, Fred and myself all got into Dr Ingram's car, which was standing in the yard, and let the brake off. We rolled straight into one of the chestnut trees which were at the side of the yard. Did we get into trouble? Plus Dr Ingram had to do his calls on foot! My dad's wage with the Ingham family was £3.00 a week. Later Dr Darke came to the manor house and after he left it was badly neglected and went to ruin. Gardens that my father had worked in for so many years all became overgrown. It was heartbreaking to see it all."

Contributor: Mrs KE Cook.

The Development of Humberstone

"The first developments were on Vicarage Lane, then Humberstone Drive by Browning Brothers in 1928. Stanley Drive was built by Carr's the builders and named after their son Stanley, who I knew. The Trocadero Cinema was built by Bert Cole on what was the "Aeroplane" field (one had force landed there in the 1920's). Scraptoft Lane was developed by Bert Cole and Sherrifs principally. Bert Cole also built the "Lido" near Brookside Tennis Courts - this is now Goodwood Bowling

Club. Humberstone Park was made from the house and grounds belonging to the Evans who were millers in Leicester. As a boy I remember I was taken by my mother to have tea in the house with Mrs Evans, this house is now the cafe."

Vicarage Lane. Early 1920's

"When my father was demobbed in 1923 after 24 years in the army he decided he would like to live in Humberstone where a lot of new properties were being built. He commuted his pension as a Regimental Sargeant Major and signed for a house costing £625 on the old Humberstone Hall estate which had been sold by the Paget family for development. We hadn't a great deal of furniture at the time as we had been living in Glen Parva barracks so had to expend more money to start furnishing it. It had only two bedrooms, an outside toilet and coal house and a small bathroom to which you pumped the water from a boiler in the small kitchen below it. There was room at the side of the house for a garage and quite a good sized lawn on the front and a very large back garden. Our new address was now "Home View", Stanley Drive, Humberstone. We lived halfway up Stanley Drive which stretched almost to Humberstone village. To our rear was the top end of Pine Tree Avenue. I seemed to live in wellingtons all the time as the roads were unmade and a quagmire in winter."

"My stay in Humberstone started in 1926 when my parents moved into one of the newly built houses (by Browning Brothers, a local builder), on the south east side of Humberstone Drive (the odd numbers). The Drive was then a county boundary for city and county. The even numbers were in the city, and the odd numbers in the county. No footpaths were made up on the county side of the Drive, no street lights, only a horse and cart (the muck cart) to collect the household rubbish for the county dwellers. What a joy to have the benefit of low county rates!

The corner of Thurmaston Lane. Early 1920's

In the immediate neighbourhood, Greenland Drive was a tree lined track. Thurmaston Lane between Humberstone Drive and Gipsy Lane was a footpath forming one side of the triangle known as Crow's Orchard, and Overton Road (now Wycombe Road) between Humberstone Drive and Victoria Road East was a track called the Black Pad.

Alas, Humberstone was soon swallowed up by the city - footpaths made up on the "odds" side of Humberstone Drive and gas lamps installed - two advantages of progress! Trees were felled in Greenland Drive and a new road surface made. But what a shock for the "odds" now having to pay City rates! We wondered if we could afford progress.

I walked to school every day from Humberstone Drive to the top end of Main Street passing the thatched cottage and grounds owned by the late Mr Wale, the oil merchant, perhaps stopping to feed the horses in his paddock. This disappeared 28 years ago and has been replaced by houses flanking Hayling Crescent - conservation having come too late. On past the builder's yard owned by Bert Cole. At the side of this yard was an alleyway leading up to the cottages which were once the homes of gardeners employed at Humberstone Hall (an uncle of mine once worked there). This builder's yard is now replaced by flats - Cedar Court - although the yew trees that fronted the yard still survive.

Rose Cottage, Humberstone Drive. 1923

On again passing Rose Cottage, a thatched cottage, very attractive but long since demolished to become the car park for the Constitutional Club at the corner of Main Street. On up the hill of Main Street passing the small chapel that later became the library, a favourite of generations of Humberstone folk and the subject of much concern when closed having been condemned as being unsafe - years later still standing and in use as a stationer's business. I then passed by Browning Brothers builders yard, now a courtyard of retirement flats. I usually called for friends living in a courtyard of cottages with a communal water pump in the middle of the yard. These were situated at the back of the thatched cottage which still stands at the corner of Main Street and Tennis Court Drive. The cottages long since demolished and the site now occupied by two pairs of semi-detached houses."

"This was a new development and there was no main sewer, but each house had a cesspool at the bottom of the back garden. This was emptied each week by a big tank which came round. Sometimes the cesspools would overflow and the smell was terrible."

"The Garden City was run on the Co-op method, all supposed to make it pay, but it didn't work, no such thing as water closets, we had to bury it in the garden."

Contributors: BM Purdy, Mrs BI Roberts, GAP Allen, Mrs JE Brewin, Mrs H Rimmington.

Childhood

"Humberstone played a great part in my life, the fields and trees with wild flowers, violets, and buttercups were part of its charm."

"Sometimes having an excess of energy, a few of us climbed the nearby sandpit, where old tin trays were hidden under the low branches of trees. Older boys had long ago grooved a slide down to the bottom. We hurtled down in turn, shrieking and half paralysed with fear. Near the bottom a tree root caught the edge of our trays, tipping us over. The boys were very clever in jumping clear, but I never did. The sandpit was expressly forbidden me - denials were useless when I arrived home late with sandy patches on the seat of my knickers."

Looking down Main Street from Thurmaston Lane crossroads. Early 1920's

"There was a walnut tree which we used to watch till we thought it was ready to be raided. If you don't know, there is a greenish pulpy skin covering the walnut shell. After one of our raids we were in school and the headmaster was walking round the class as he very often did and stopped along side my pal Ted and asked if his dad knew he was smoking. Ted denied smoking and the headmaster said, well why are your fingers all stained, go to the front of the class. He got three strokes of the cane on his hands. Ted couldn't admit he had been stealing walnuts or the headmaster would have told his parents and he would have been in more trouble."

"Up Main Street into the village stood the Plough Inn and I can remember as a small boy, being sent to fetch a pint of beer in the bottle, carrying it tightly in the bag and they used to put a small bit of paper over the cork which should act as a seal against it being drunk by anyone under age, which today seems a bit ridiculous as the seal used to fall off as soon as it was put in the bag."

"Me dad had a bit of a smallholding. He had pigs and geese and all that, chickens and the like. He used to ride motorcycle sidecar, because with me not being at school (because of illness) I used to be with me dad all the while, everyday I was with him, and me mother, I learnt me cookin' that way. I was lucky we always seemed to have plenty of money and food. I could go down into the cellar, which was like a big scullery and me dad would have sides of pig hangin' up, all home cured. Me mum would send down with a knife and I'd cut what I wanted off. In 1942 we had a family of evacuees from London. The Solly family. I remember Annie one of the eldest daughters always used to take me hand and take me down opposite Portway, there used to a toy shop there and always buy me a couple of soldiers. Me mother would give her some money to buy me a couple of soldiers. She'd be getting on for her seventies now."

Contributors: Mrs E Politoske, Mrs L Wakelin, JE Cook, Mr Stevens, Mr Derek.

School

"Morning prayers were taken by the vicar, the Reverend Eric Farrar. The bell from the old school is now in St Elizabeth's Church and I still think of my school days when I hear it ring on Sunday mornings. On hot summer days we had our lessons under the lime trees at the back of the church."

"I went to Humberstone C.E. School in the village, the only schooling I had, it consisted of two teachers a Mr. Clarke and Miss Cort, it was a dreadful place, so cold, just a stove and nothing else, we had to clap our hands to get some warmth and the toilets were just pits, no water."

"At the "new School" in Humberstone all the boys in the top classes had allotments in the school grounds allocated to them, two boys to each, where we were instructed in gardening as a lesson. I think the girls did sewing."

Humberstone School - Girls with Mr Clarke and Miss Cort. Boys with Mr Clarke. 1914. (Kindly loaned by Mrs H Rimmington)

"Mr Clarke was like a kindly uncle, always finding the best in his pupils. His elderly open-topped car trundled along, stopping at each group of children. "Anyone for Stanley Drive?" he'd call. Those of us for Stanley Drive clambered on to the running board and into the back, not bothering with doors. We piled on top of the squashy leather seat, and each other, giggling and laughing. The traffic free Main Street allowed a slight increase in speed up to Lewin's corner, where we were told to "Hold on tight!" Outside Mr Clarke's house, his "Goodbye children, be careful!" was answered by a chorus of "Goodbye sir! Thank you" whilst dutifully looking left and right."

"Polly" Bracken knew everything! With no aids to textbooks other than blackboard and chalk, she switched subjects effortlessly. Long division, English grammer, rainfall of the world, the Norman Conquest, Walter - de-la-Mare's poetry were all absorbed with respectful attention. But the singing classes saw us really letting off steam. We stood belting out "The Wedding of the Painted Doll" accompanied by rattling tambourines and tinkling triangles.

My class was once told to write out a story read the previous week. I tried in vain to say that I had not been at school that day. Jack the kindhearted boy sharing my desk, nudged my ribs. "Just copy mine," he whispered. So I did. I copied his name too!."

"I remember the school outing to Windsor one May Saturday in 1938. We travelled by special train to Bourne End and boarded a river steamer. On arrival at Windsor we were trailed at speed through St George's Chapel and parts of the castle. I recall the efforts made by some to try to make the unblinking sentries smile. Prior to leaving Windsor by train we had tea in a hut at Eton. Eton boys in their frock coats and top hats were a source of amusement to us, particularly the one carrying his tin of peas under his arm as he raised his hat to someone."

Childrens Annual Christmas Party held in the Church rooms. On the left is Mrs Taylor and on the right with the hat, Miss Wheatley. The children are Beryl Chapman, Betty Philpot. Ellen, Jean Weston and Margaret. (Kindley loaned by Beryl Skelton (nee Chapman))

"Now the memories of school start to come back. My first teacher was Miss Attenborough, and the Infant School was the wooden building at the back of the school. I'm afraid I didn't like her very much because she made fun of me and made me stand at the front of the class because I couldn't thread a needle. It was found out later I had poor eyesight and needed glasses.

The one teacher I remember the most was Miss Bracken, I was about 10-11 when she taught me, and the main subjects she taught were music, English and poetry. I still remember the quite difficult songs she taught us, pieces from the Messiah and Gilbert and Sullivan operas. She was very strict, but I've never forgotten the things she taught, especially the poems.

Another teacher we had reason to remember was Mr Smith, who taught us the following year (I think). He used to walk round with a big ruler, I can't remember him ever using it on a pupil, but he used it to slam down on the desk to get silence, also he used to slam the lid of his desk down with such force, the hinge would break. The woodwork master was always having to repair it. I think Miss Bracken and Mr Smith married. Mr Palmer taught the senior boys. Mr Clarke was the headmaster. He always seemed quite nice, but woe betide any pupil that was sent to his office for misbehaving, it was generally the cane.

I remember the cookery classes in our last year. Nothing I made ever turned out right. My toffee never set, my bread was as heavy as lead and even the cat wouldn't eat the potato and onion soup I took home. But I enjoyed the housewifery side, the old flat irons that had to be heated on the coal or coke stoves. On the whole I enjoyed my days at Humberstone School."

Contributors: CJ Freeman, Mrs H Rimmington, BM Purdy, Mrs L Wakelin, GAE Gray, Mrs D Tomlinson.

Work

"When I first came to live in Leicester, my first place here was as a maid to a couple who had just had a house built in the Pine Tree Avenue... From this house I moved to a double fronted house on the corner of Humberstone Drive, which was the residence of the proprieter of Carr's Fever Powders in Wharf Street."

"When the first war broke out, we had to go to work, 13 years old and catch the tram at the terminus, out at work and only two sandwiches for the day, as regards entertainment, we were too tired."

House at the corner of Uppingham Road and Humberstone Drive (Kindly loaned by Mrs J E Brewin)

"I left school at 13 years (1917) and went to work for a farmer - Mr Ambrose Rouse at Elms Farm. I went on the milk round in the mornings which covered from Humberstone Village to Nedham Street. I remember Mrs Pilsworth at the shop in Vulcan Road, she used to give me a piece of cake when I delivered the milk. On cattle market days, Ambrose would catch a tram on the Humberstone Road and leave me to drive the milk float back to the farm. In the afternoons I would help on the farm with general farm work or in the ploughed fields leading horses and chain-harrowing. Elms farm farmhouse is now part of the Hamilton Estate."

"The village blacksmith, Mr Mason, had premises opposite the old church hall. Many a time we would stop on the way home from school to see Mr Mason at work, heating the iron bars in his forge and shaping it on his anvil to make horse shoes. Later to see him manoeuvre the leg of a shire horse on to his lap and to place the hot horse shoe on the hoof with the hiss and smell of burning hoof, prior to hammering into place with large horse shoe nails."

Contributors: Mrs JE Brewin, Mrs H Rimmington, CJ Freeman, GAP Allen.

Shopping

"Shopping was lovely. I used to do all my shopping at Allison's and I used to take my order in and it was delivered to me. Now we have to carry it. They were lovely people. The sub-post office was in the shop. A grand old boy Bill Russell was a veteran of the Great War. We all mingled in together."

Allison's the grocer's and Post Office. The picture on page 4 shows the same street, but before the shop front was changed. (Kindly loaned by Mr & Mrs Falstead)

"On the way to school was a really great sweet shop that sold every sweet a child could ask for. Mr Hall used to be so patient with the children, there was a box for them to stand on, and what a treat it was to to stand and choose something to spend your halfpenny on."

"Across the road from the Plough was a row of shops with steps up into the cold stone floors. One of them had a huge soft drinks machine that stood on the counter, I believe it was called Vantas, and I will always remember this thing, sort of a huge bubble would emerge from the bottom as it bubbled up and poured out and mixed a drink for children. It always amazed me this thing and I imagine I stood open mouthed watching the bubble burst."

"The shops in the village in the 1930's began with Mr Pick's cobbler's shop and was followed by Mrs Underwood's grocery and sweet shop. Across the road was Mr Mason's blacksmith's forge, followed by Jack King the hairdresser. Next door was Rose Vyse, a ladies' outfitting and wool shop. This was followed by Hall's sweetshop and how we loved to go in there. Mr Walter Bartram was the butcher next door and what a cheerful man he was. The post office and grocery near the corner of Vicarage Lane was owned by Mr Simpkin and was later taken over by Mr Allison. The two public houses in the village were The Plough Inn whose landlord was Arthur Cayless and across the road was the Windmill Inn whose landlord was Mr Salmon and he was followed by Fergie Johnson."

At the back of Pick's the cobblers with "Young Mr Pick" and Kathleen and Rosemary Falstead. The wooden box on the wall was used for storing meat before fridges became common. (Kindly loaned by Mr & Mrs Falstead)

Contributors: Mr & Mrs Felstead, Mrs D Tomlinson, Mr Stevens, D Bryan.

Events

"The Annual Garden Fete was a big event, everyone used to turn out for that. Mr and Mrs Turner who lived at the large house called the Warren used to open their grounds for it. There was always the fancy dress parade led by a band, and the horse drawn floats. There was Mrs Walton, Mrs Taylor, Mrs Avons and Mrs Smith. I was in it one year on Mrs Walton's float, we were a band of gypsies, and there was Mary Spittal, Dorothy Laudon and myself as children sat round the camp fire in the centre. Mrs Smith was the old woman who lived in a shoe and Mrs Avons was Will Hay etc."

"I remember the garden fete, it was held where the road runs through now, up behind the church. There used to be some wrought iron gates there and a beautiful gravel path and lawned gardens where the fete was held."

St Mary's Church. After the 2nd World War

"My chapel, Humberstone Road Congregational, had a thousand scholars and the light of our lives was the school treat. With the Salvation Army band we walked to the fields at Humberstone, had a picnic and games and walked home. I remember the horse trams changing horses at the top of the hill by Forest Road, a little Japanese Garden somewhere around Gipsy Lane which later moved to Aylestone."

"I can remember in 1935 Sir Oswald Mosley's Blackshirts holding a meeting in the village one evening. One of the youths began to barrack them and finished up on his knees saying he was sorry. The village lads were about eight to their twenty or so."

"Old Humberstone "Flower Show" was a big yearly event. It was held in the church rooms always in August, and there was a special class for children to show a jar of wild flowers. We had plenty around the village, so it was good fun going into the fields to collect wild flowers and put them into our jam jars. I guess there was a small prize for the best, I can't remember, but they did look lovely. There was always a lot of rivalry amongst our dads with vegetables, fruit and flowers. The village parson took a keen interest in all the village events and you could be sure he would always arrive just as cups of tea were about. The good old days!"

Contributors: Mrs B Skelton, Mr Stevens, Mrs E Politoske, JE Cook, Mrs KE Cook

---

Entertainment

"Come to 1936 my two friends and I were pushing on for our 18th birthdays and we fancied our chances as budding Fred Astaires, on a Tuesday night we would board a bus at the Shaftsbury Cinema that would take us all the way to Old Humberstone Garden City for 1.1/2d old money, we would enter Laburnham Hall on payment of 6d and we would dance to the best dance bands in the country (on records of course) and at the interval we had a free cup of tea and two biscuits, then at 10.30 a 1.1/2d ride back to the Shaftsbury, all this made a lovely night out for nine pence."

"I remember the old Trocadero Cinema going up - what excitement, a picture house at the bottom of our road! ...We used to have two feature films, the Pathe news and sometimes a little variety show in between - what value for money. There was a ballroom upstairs where, when in my teens I went for ballroom dancing lessons and later to proper dances!

"The British Legion was over the corner shop on Vicarage Lane, afterwards it moved to the corner of Pine Tree Avenue. Many happy times there, always a flower show, baby competitions and beauty queen, women's section, jam and home made wines etc."

"When my first daughter was married we just had a sandwich do. Because we lived just across the road (from the old Plough Inn), I went across for a bottle of wine, I think. He said to me, "what have you going off Tom?" " I've got a wedding." He said,"how are you getting that lot in there?" He called his wife and said,"get the keys and unlock that and let Tom have the lounge, he's got a wedding over there." She said,"I told you his daughter was getting married". Do you know, It never cost me a penny in the end. We got some of our own, but he kept coming in and saying, "What do you want?" - of course he was drunk. Our room had a tiny little window over the centre at the top. You could see the old Plough Inn written on the wall opposite. If I didn't go to the pub over the other side of the road to the old Plough he used to come and bring me a pint and shove it through the window to me."

"Church was very popular in my youth. I joined the choir and it involved morning and evening service and practise for an hour Friday evening. One Friday I was helping haymaking on a farm at the top of Keyham Lane when I heard the church bell ringers begin their practise, I hurried down to church and was about 8-9 minutes late. Mr Burton the choirmaster scowled at me and said he'd see me later. Choir practice finished and Mr Burton said,"right lads, line up for the quarterly payment." When my turn came he told me to wait till last when he asked why I had been late. I said I had been helping a farmer. Well you can wait until next quarter as you kept me waiting to practise the choir before you get your money! But the following Friday he gave me my money - 3s 6d only 17 1/2 pence now, but quite a lot then.

Humberstone Choral Society, taken in the front garden of Miss Shepherd's house next to the Church. Miss Shepherd is in the front row with the hat. (Kindly loaned by Mrs H Rimmington)

"The church rooms were the centre of all events. Sunday school was there, whist drives, meetings, the British Legion had their children's party there and lots more. The 1st Humberstone Girl Guides was formed there, of which I was one of the first to join. At the back of the church rooms, there was a wooden hut. You went up steps to get in it. It was here just before the 1939 war that four of us founded the 65th Leicester Cub Scout Group. For many years we carried on, now the 65th meet at the scout hut in Wigley Road."

"When I was about twelve, the sunday school formed a concert party called the NITWITS, which I was a member of. It was a bit amateurish, but we had a lot of fun and raised money for the church."

"We also had a very good football team called Humberstone St Mary's. It was managed by Tommy Ansell whose son was a very good centre forward. The goal keeper was Fred Shilton who became uncle to Peter Shilton. Any bumps and bruises would be dealt with by the local doctor, Dr Ingham who lived in the Manor House."

Contributors: H Limbert, Mrs E Chesterton, Mrs D Larkins, Mr & Mrs Falstead, JE Cook, Mrs KE Cook, Mrs D Tomlinson, D Bryan.

Characters

"The Reverend Percy Lidster (or uncle Percy as he was known to us young ones). He was a grand man and always ready to help or give advice when needed, even at our wedding when one of the choir boys was late, and was hurrying up the aisle, he made a joke about it which caused a titter amongst the guests. Fred Smith's mother was the village character, she was midwife, nurse, layer-out etc: if anyone needed help send for Mrs Smith...she was rather stout and used to stand outside her house, arms folded and her pinny on."

"One character well known was Billy Wood the son of the milkman who lived in Steins Lane, Billy had a good singing voice but had a cleft pallet which made him difficult to understand and children tended to rib him."

"I remember the procession down to the fete being led by a local character, I believe his name was Bill Wood, who walked with a limp and sported a Charlie Chaplin bowler hat and walking cane."

"Another character used to be, he used to play cricket with us, Sam Cook. I don't know what disease he had, he were shaking and mumbling all the time, but on the Humberstone Park there off Keyham Lane he used to play cricket with us and he were good and he enjoyed it. We turned out to be good friends after that, amazing isn't it, yet we were all frightened of him before."

"My father-in-law had quite a large garden and at one time kept a sow in a sty opposite the school but every time the children had singing lessons, the pig would come out of her sty, put her two front feet up on the garden wall, look over to the school and make a terrible racket until the headmaster came across saying "can't you keep that pig quiet?" Thereafter it was known as the "Singing Pig"."

Contributors: Mrs B Skelton, BM Purdy, Mr Stevens, Mr Derek, Mrs M Sherriff.

West Humberstone and the Uppingham Road

"Maundy Thursday was the day I decided to make my entrance into the world at the Moore family home in Morton Road, West Humberstone, where my mother had lived since 1901 and from where, two days later on Easter Saturday her younger brother was to be married. As usual the entire family would gather, but the house was used to this. It wasn't long since another brother had left to be married and also an elder sister, husband and three babies had left to live two streets away. In addition the front room had been used as a hat shop! Now there would just be grandad, my parents and me.

A pity my mother would have to miss the wedding, but the local "unqualified" midwife, Mrs Marlow would make sure she spent her full time in bed! Two years later she was to deliver mum a still-born son who was put into a shoe box and given to dad to take to the incinerator. How times change.

In 1930 my baby sister arrived at the time of the whooping cough epidemic (no injections then) and this must be my first memory, being taken along the Portway - just being built- to a tar van on Uppingham Road. The men expected us and lifted us up to inhale the fumes, a sure cure, and also soaked a piece of rope which when cool was hung around our necks.

Most of the children around us went to Merridale School, but I was sent along with my cousins to St Barnabas School where we diligently learnt our catechism and regularly went into the church on Saints Days. To see us safely across Uppingham Road was a lovely fat policeman and always in the playground was the curate Reverend Strudwick to chat with us. From the age of three I should think that all the children in the neighbourhood went to Sunday School at West Humberstone Gospel Mission in Brighton Road. My parents met there, I met my husband there and my paternal grandfather who was a founder met his wife there too.

On Sunday School anniversary day we were crammed on to the specially erected platform and it was always so hot. In spite of the poverty everyone seemed to sport a new dress or shirt. The singing was splendid, the crowds came, it was wonderful. On Monday evening we received our prizes of books and bibles for good attendance - 75 marks for third prize, 85 for a second and 95 for a first. Then there was the Sunday school treat. We walked in snake like procession from Brighton Road to Humberstone Road Station and boarded a train for Sileby. Then another walk to the field for games, races and lucky bags and an orange. Oh yes, and tea in the local Methodist Church. The potted meat sandwiches were delicious!

School holidays were all fun, even though mostly spent on the parks. Special treats were a penny return on the train from Humberstone Station to Belgrave Road and then the short walk to Abbey Park. Or a ride on two trams to Western Park, but of course Sparrow Park and Humberstone Park were most frequently the venues.

Then there was the backyard concert our family used to arrange. One year I got to be the May Queen with a crown made of white hedgerow blossom and dog roses and one of Mum's net curtains for a train. We sang, danced and acted our hearts out and used the lavatory at the bottom of the yard as our changing room. Admission was a half-penny or two buttons and the audience got sandwiches and cakes and a drink. What value!

The street parties for the 1935 Jubilee and 1937 Coronation were real highlights, everyone in fancy dress, even the grown ups. Streamers across the streets, usually made out of old rags dyed appropriately red, white and blue and made into flags. Tables borrowed from the mission and running the length of the street, filled to overflowing with goodies and prizes for everyone. What fun we had at election times too. A local conservative owned some of the houses in our street and used to send a car to pick up the tenants, taking them to the polling stations (not that they voted Tory) and we used to chase the cars and sing rude songs. It was great. There was an abbatoir on Victoria Road East and it was not unusual to see the blood being swilled from the pavement. Also I don't know why but occasionally a bull would be driven along our road. We were warned by the ringing of a handbell and doors were locked and entry gates securely closed, that is if you had one!

Then there was Curly, the ice-cream man and poor "Silly-Billy" who we all loved really. How lovely to be able to play safely in the streets - cricket (with the stumps marked in the wall with chalk), rounders, hot rice, hop-scotch, truth, dare or promise, marbles, donkey - the list is endless. Lots of families had allotments nearby and we often had a picnic there, it was like being in the country.

One of my favourite memories is Saturday night we were given threepence, a lot of money. One penny was for the collection on Sunday, but the other two pence was spent at Pratt's sweet shop on Victoria Road East. But how to decide what to buy, the choice was endless. I usually had a half-pennyworth of four different kinds - dolly mixtures, ducks green peas and potatoes, marzipan tea cakes and sherbet fishes. Another treat was fish and chips from Doo's for three pence.

Of course there were sad times such as a death in the community which seemed to affect us all. The black board was nailed to the window of the deceased's house, a collection was taken for a wreath and every contribution carefully recorded, name and amount, and the wreath duly displayed on the day of the funeral, when as a mark of respect everyone closed their front curtains, both upstairs and down.

In contrast to this, when there was a wedding in the street, folk showed their interest, not by going to the church service, but by congregating outside the bride's house and when she and her bridesmaids emerged there were "oohs and aahs" especially from the children.

Around 1935 there was much speculation when it was announced that "the pit" (at the back of Brighton Road) was to be developed by builder Frank Craven. The place was overrun by rats etc. "The houses will never last" they said. Built they were at a cost of around £395 and today are selling for anything between £30,000 and £40,000. The lady who became my mother-in-law was employed by Mr Craven to scrub the house from top to bottom before occupation and for this she was paid the princely sum of 2/6d.

With the onset of the war in 1939 things began to change. Street lights were dimmed; schools and churches were temporarily closed until adequate air-raid shelters were built; half of our already small back yard was taken up with the brick shelter; sticky criss-cross tape appeared on the windows and yards of black material was made up into black-out curtains. The sticky tape didn't make a lot of difference when a bomb was dropped on the "Black Pad" and there were no vacuum cleaners to help clean up the mess in the house. But as always the community spirit prevailed. Frightened neighbours shared shelters; bereaved neighbours were comforted by those around and there was always the proverbial cup of tea!

These are just some of the ways I remember my part of Humberstone. I married from the same house, with the same group of people outside the door when I left, making the same exclamations. Do I miss it? Of course I do - and I am not wearing rose-coloured spectacles."

"My first recollections are of Overton Road Board School which I attended from 1925 to 1931, starting at the age of five. The teachers I can remember over the years were Miss Flint, Miss Gamble, Miss Lee, Miss Draycott, Miss Flavell. Mr Thorpe, Mr Moore and the headmaster Mr Keay, who I thought was a martinet having had a few strokes of the cane from him for talking in lines while waiting to march into school from the playground. Beyond the school which is now Tailby Estate was all allotments with a narrow path running through the middle to Humberstone Drive, Tailby Estate being built sometime around 1927. At the other end of Overton Road was the Shaftsbury Cinema (now a warehouse) where we spent a rapturous couple of hours at the "Tuppenny rush" on Saturday afternoon. It was a sight to see the lads coming out after the show running down the road being Tom Mix, Hoot Gibson or Ken Maynard, whipping their make-believe horses."

"Around the Humberstone Terminus was a comprehensive shopping area. The Pallent family ran the post office and newsagent, Mr Sim with blond quite film star-ish good looks managed the chemist's Wand's. Genial Mr Roy Gibbins was our butcher. At the corner of Turner Road was Worthington's general grocers and next door the Misses M and E Hall kept a little shop devoted to ladies underwear, hosiery and - wonderful word - haberdashery. They were quietly refined old ladies. One wore her hair in plaited earphones. They wore dresses with a white infill known

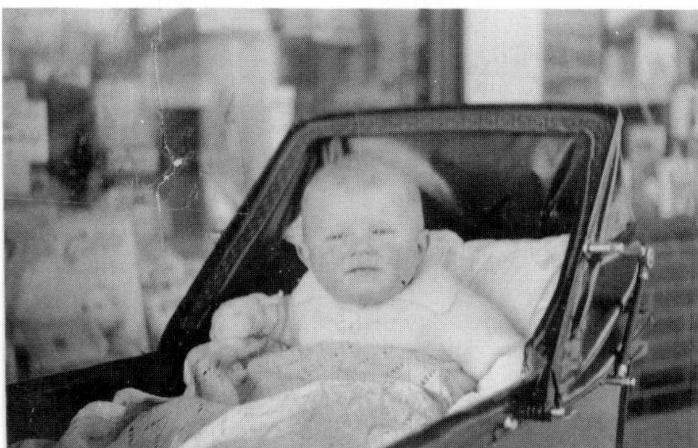

Outside Bradley's Chemist on Uppingham Road. 1936. (Kindly loaned by Mrs D Larking)

as a modesty vest. Their shop walls were lined with shallow drawers, and they would cut off as much ribbon, tape or knicker elastic as you wanted. Nothing was pre-packaged. Mr Pickard, barber also kept a small lending library and sold tobacco. Mr Newitt's hardware shop smelled like nowhere else, a mixture of fire-lighters, paraffin, creosote and polish. On December evenings we little girls would look with yearning at the grown up vanities in the window of Mary Allen, hairdresser, and make up lists of "What I would like for Christmas" - California poppy perfume, Snowfire hand-cream, Amaani shampoo, Evening in Paris... Green groceries came from the amiable Mrs Smith next door to Hill's the grocer's at the corner of Coleman Road. One of Mr Hill's assistants joined the Women's Land Army when war was declared and he himself had an attack of alopecia which fascinated us children when his hair started to grow back again in tufts of black and white - Mr Badger! We had another chemist in James L Bradley, Labour parish Councillor. In committee he fought hard with Miss Stevens, school teacher and Conservative. But these were chivalrous days and he always gave her a ride home in his car."

"At the bottom of the Martival was the railway station, with the station master's house facing East Park Road. I used to know his daughter whose name was Betty. Near the station was Humberstone Coal Wharf. We used to have to fetch the coal on Saturday morning. We would get there early to get a good barrow. We had to wait sometimes as the coal came in the railway trucks. The coalman used to bag up the coal to put in the cart, then back the cart horses up to pull the carts. Then another man served us with our coal. We used to swing on the handles of the coal barrow and the coal would sometimes tip out and we used to look like the coalmen ourselves after picking it up."

Contributors: Mrs ME Shenton, L Parsons, EJ Choice, Mrs M Chamberlain.

Humberstone Station Lamp.